HEARSTORIA

MAZE

GARDEN

BY ROCK ROULADE COCOON COLLECTIVE

This Book Belongs to:

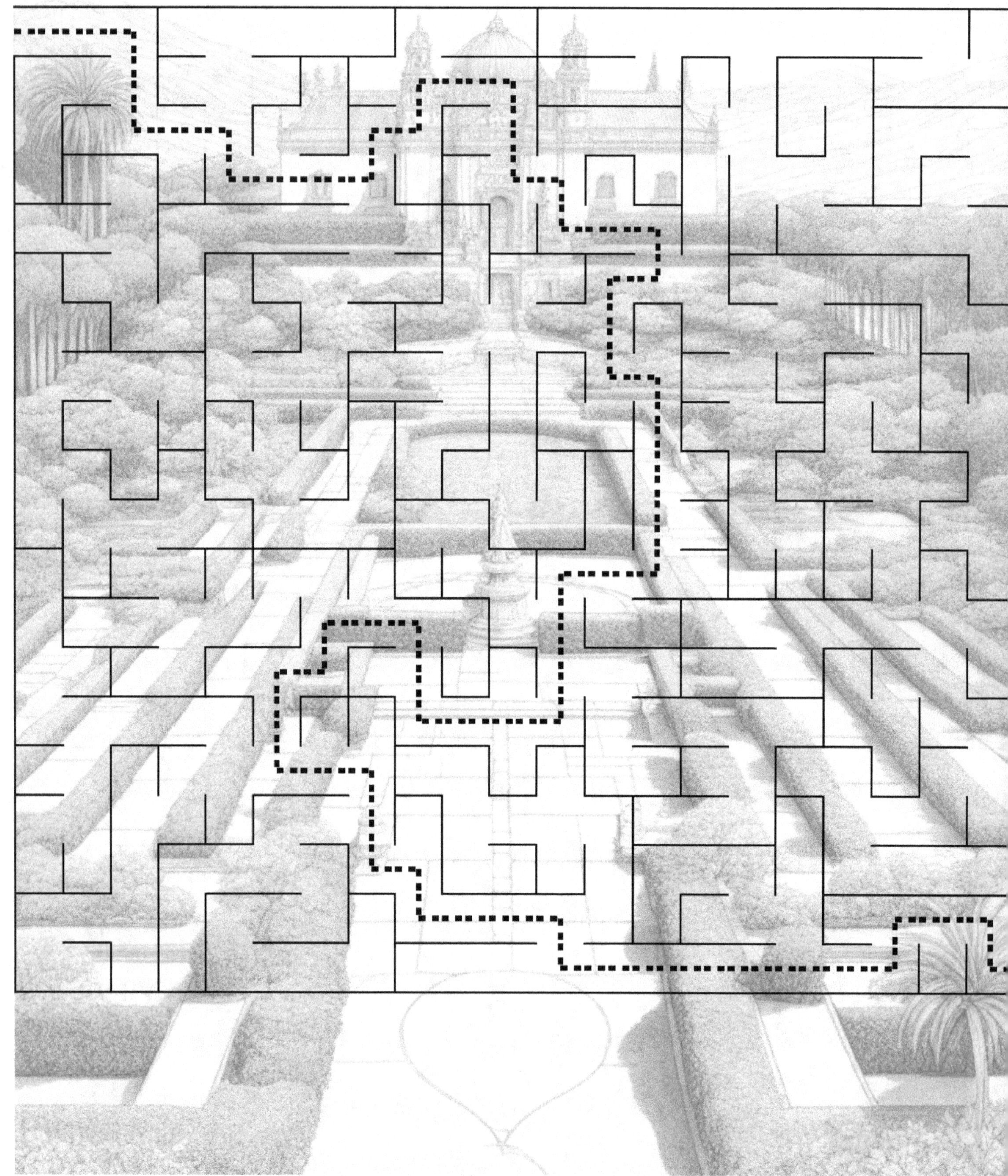

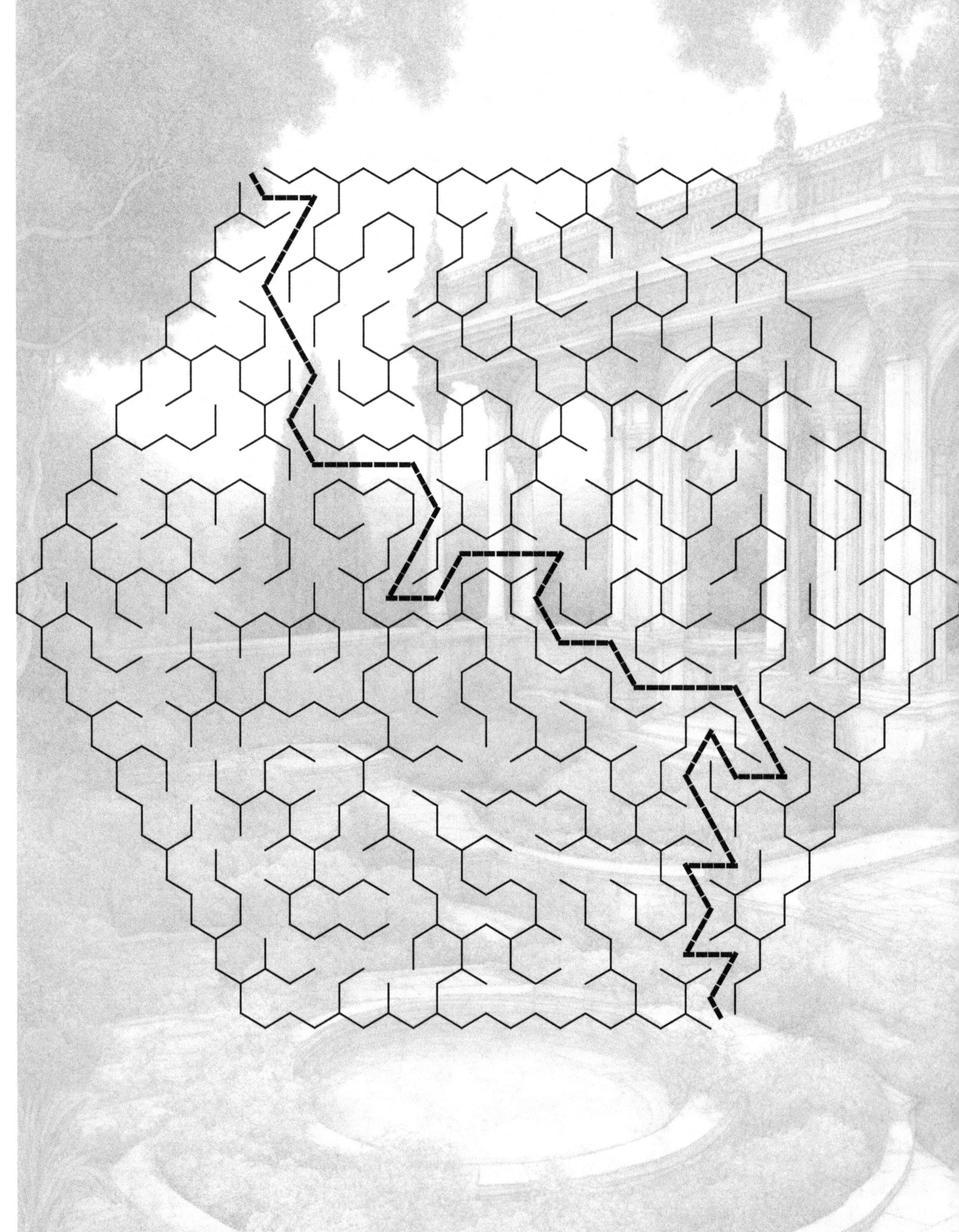

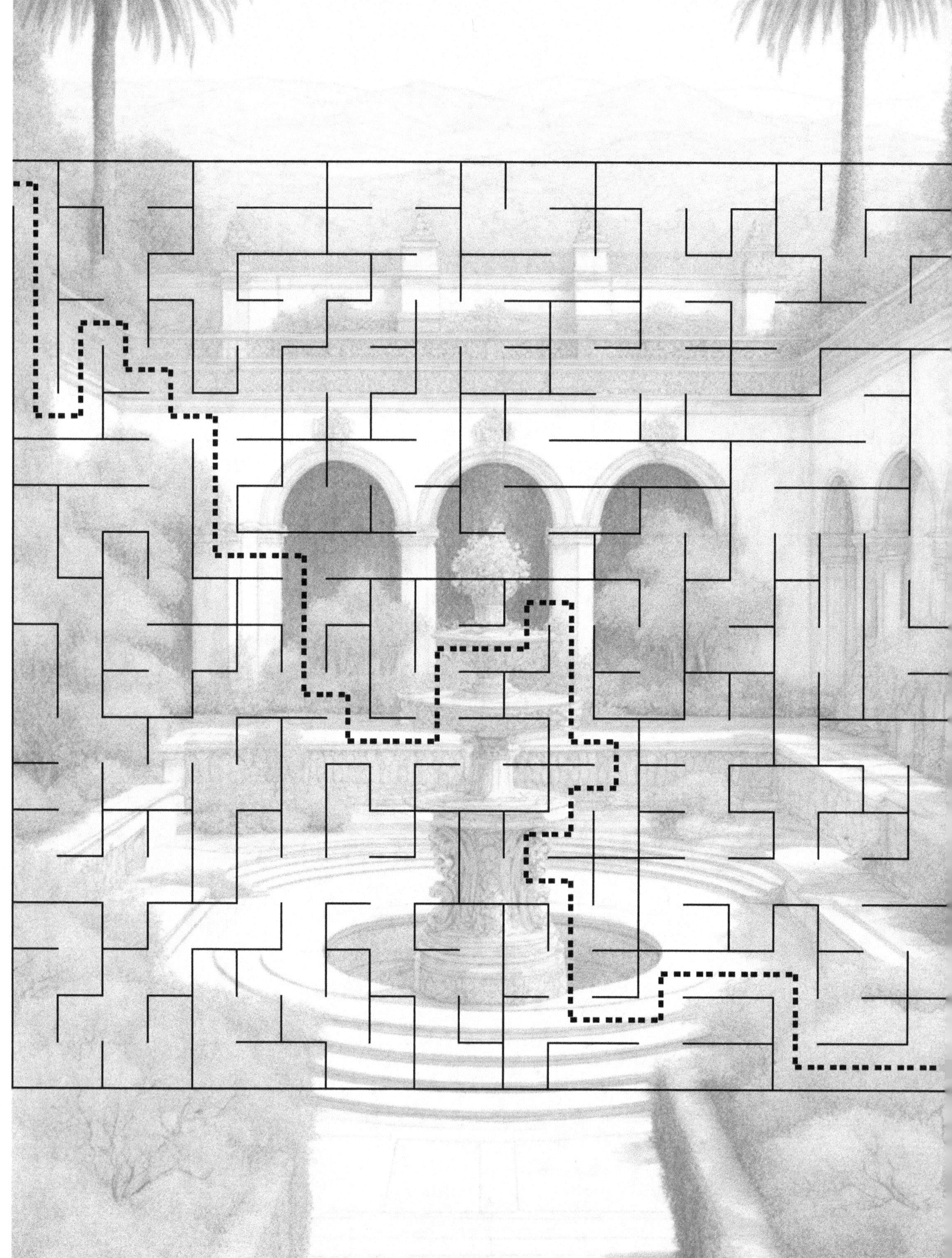

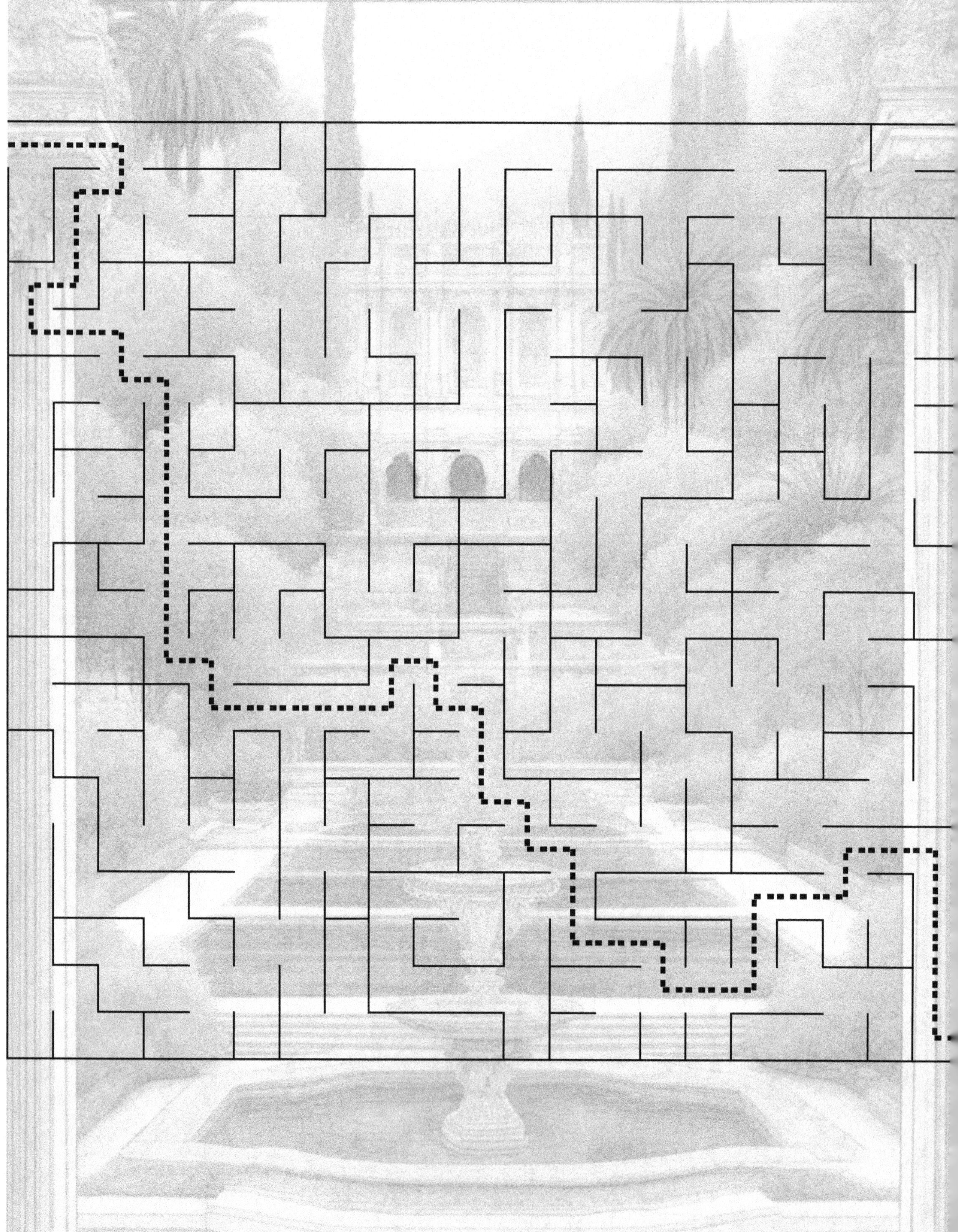

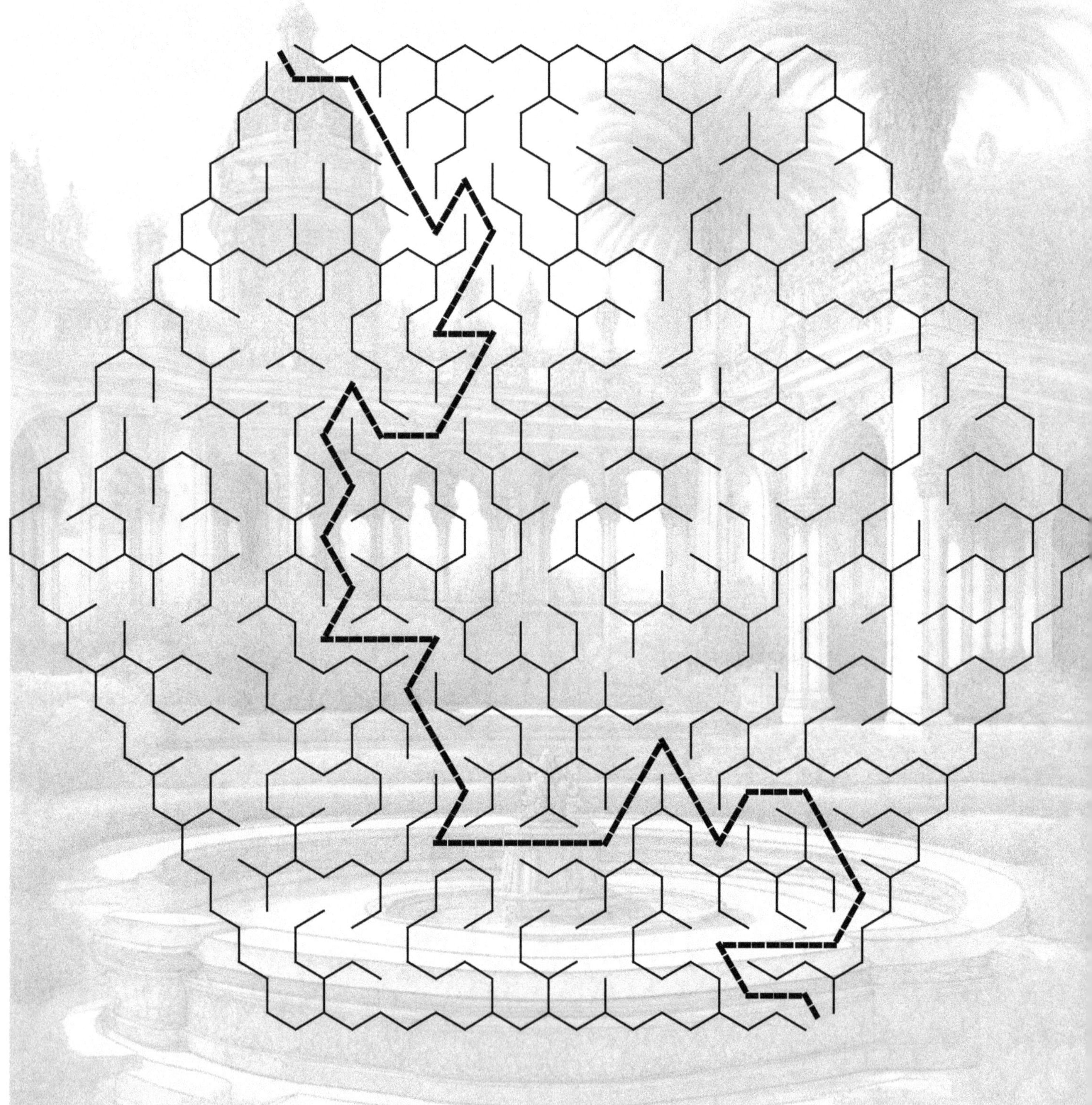

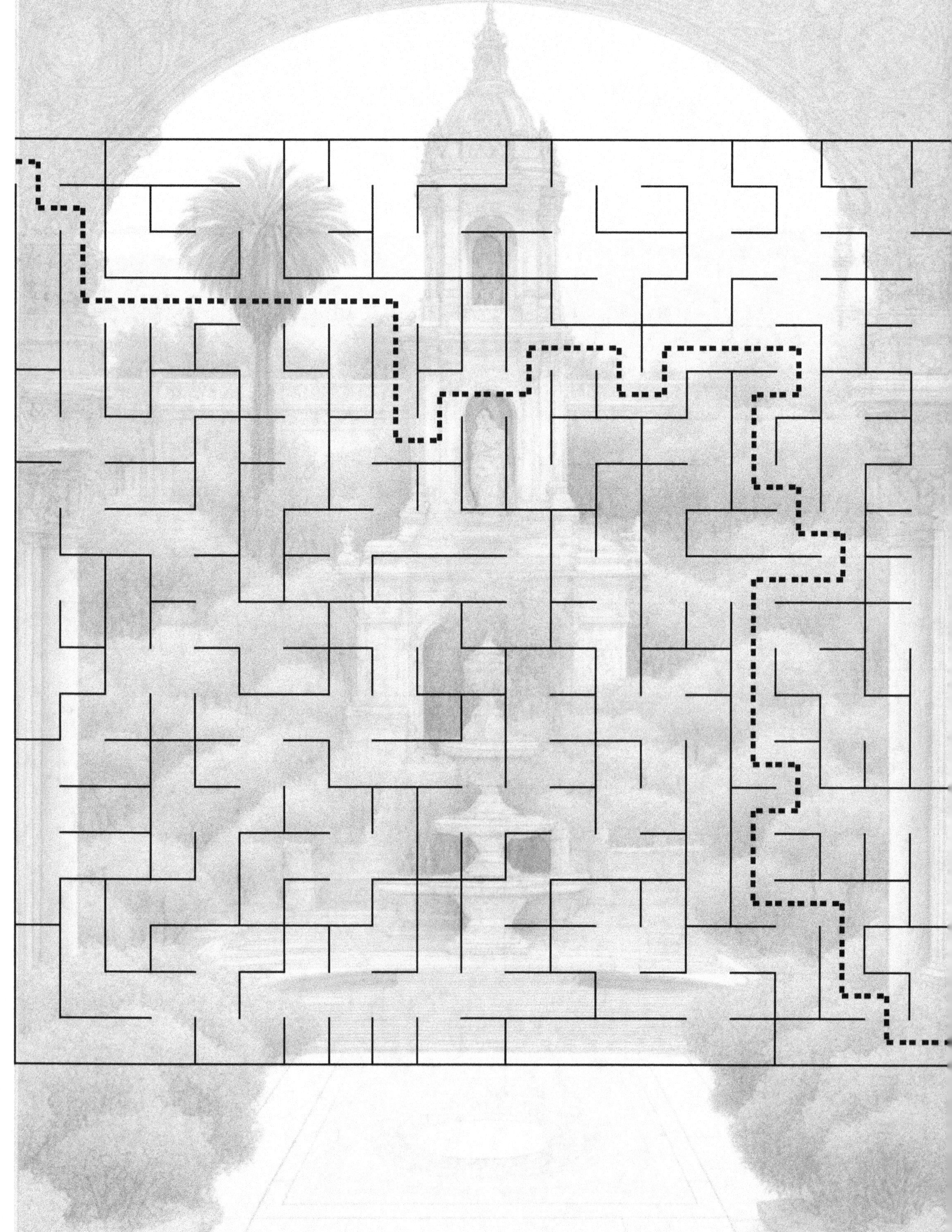

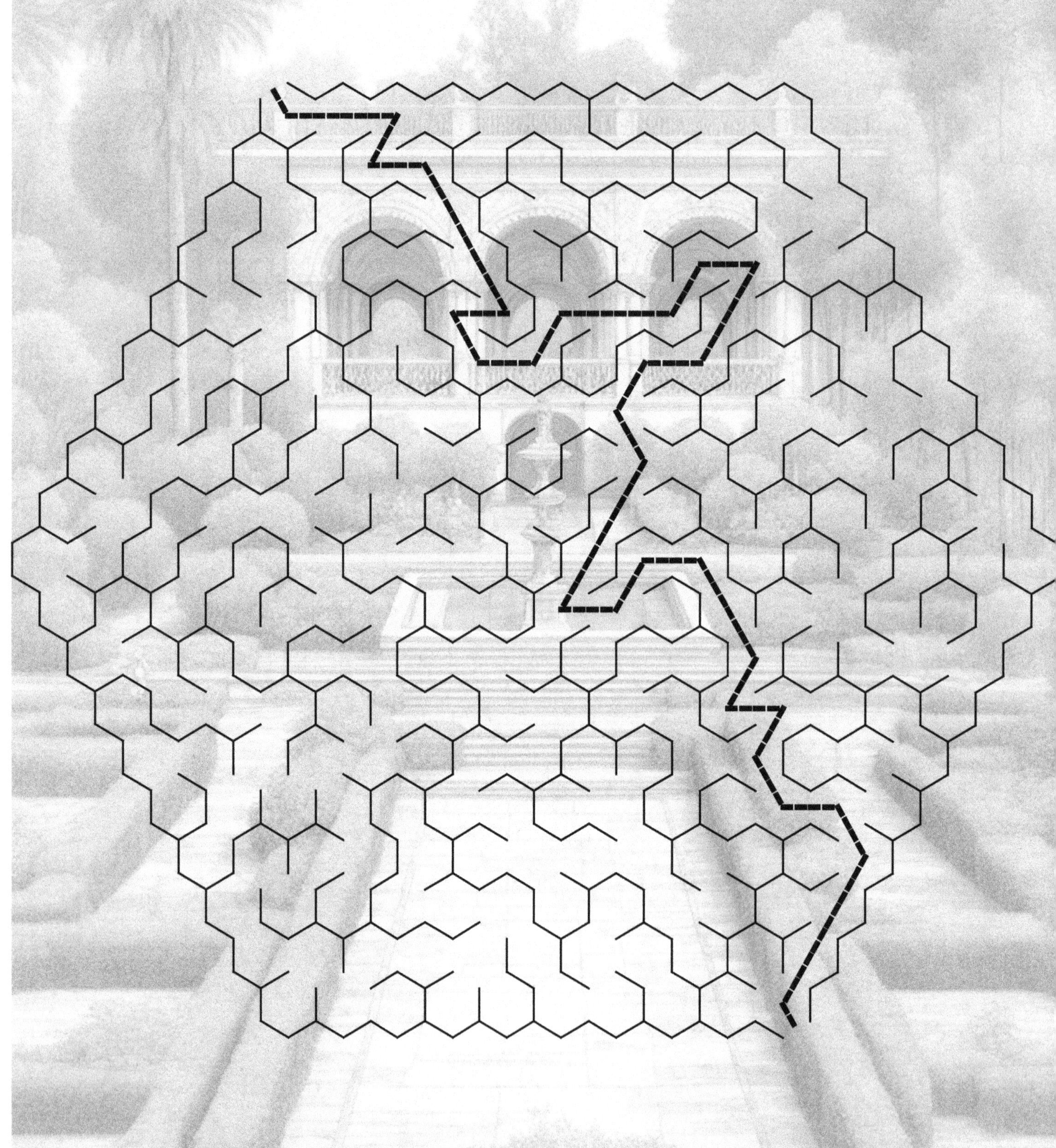

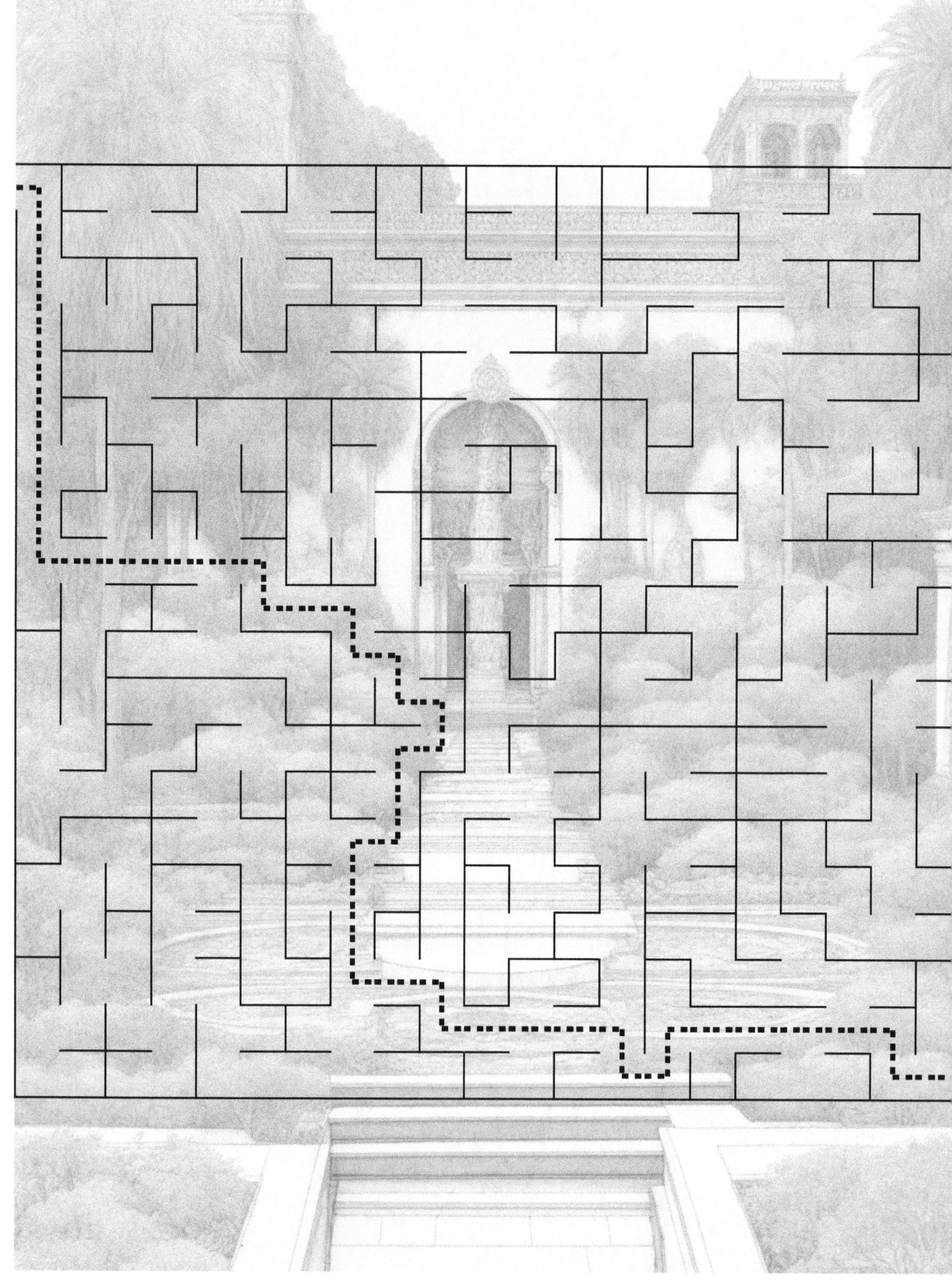

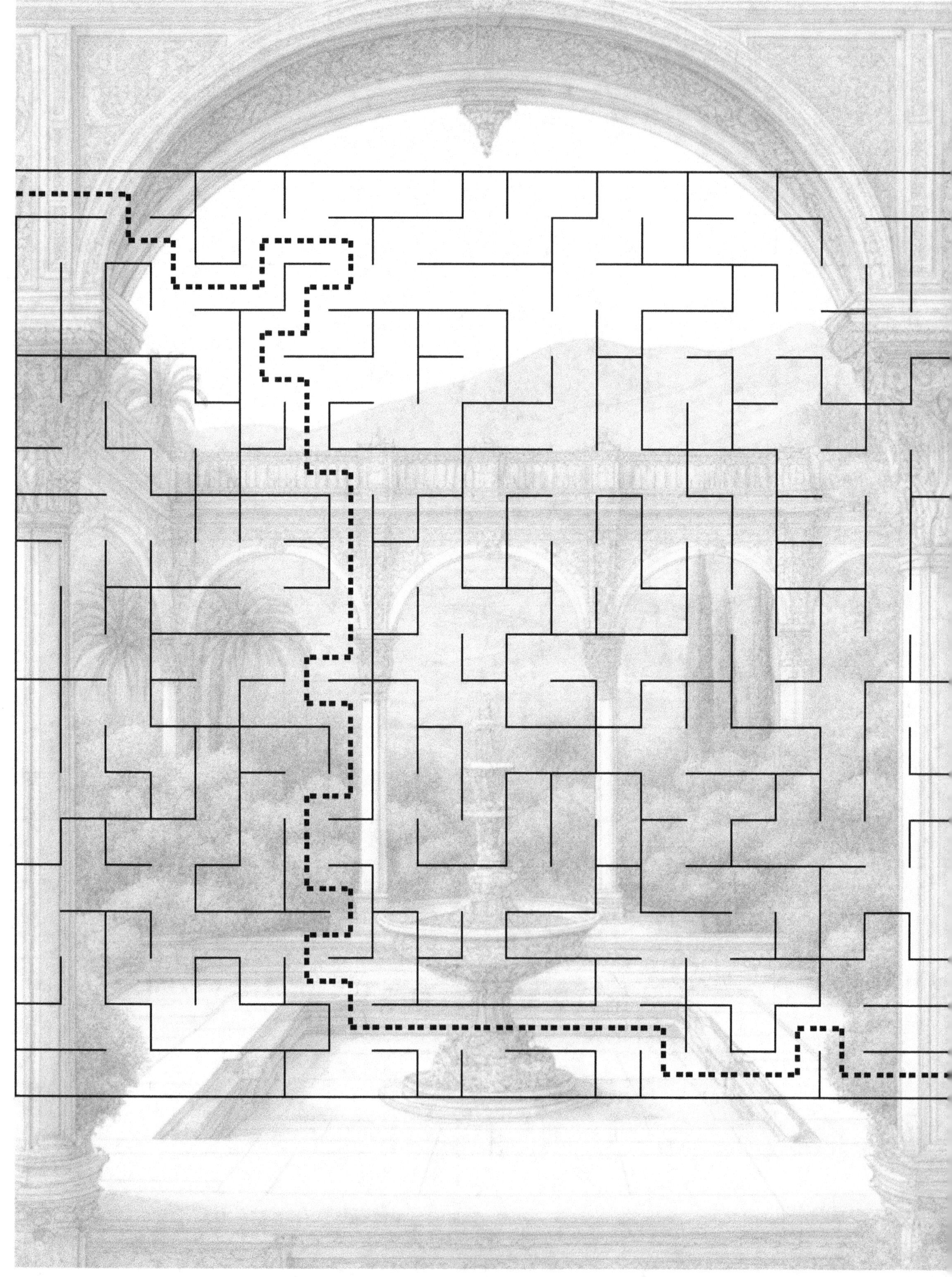

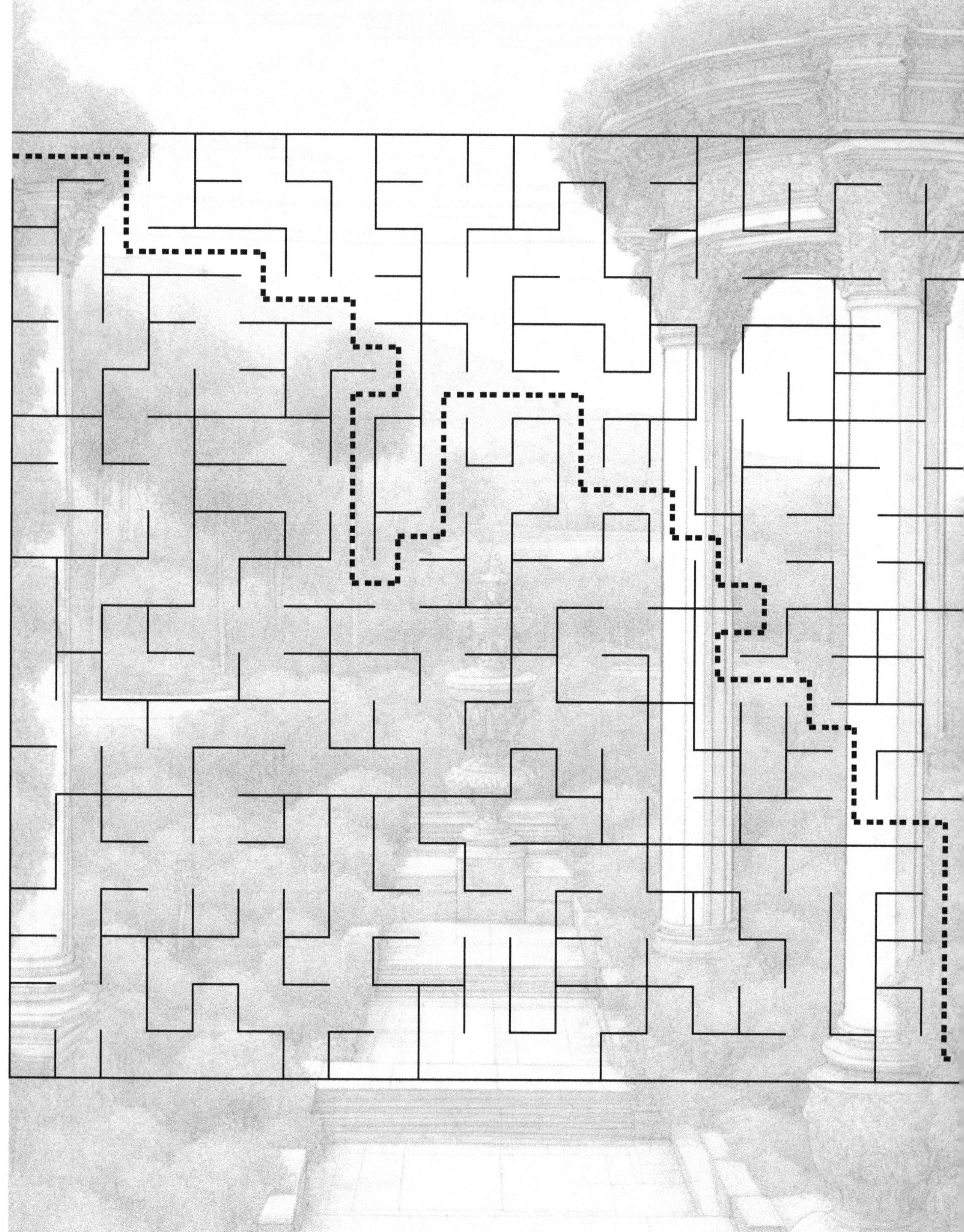

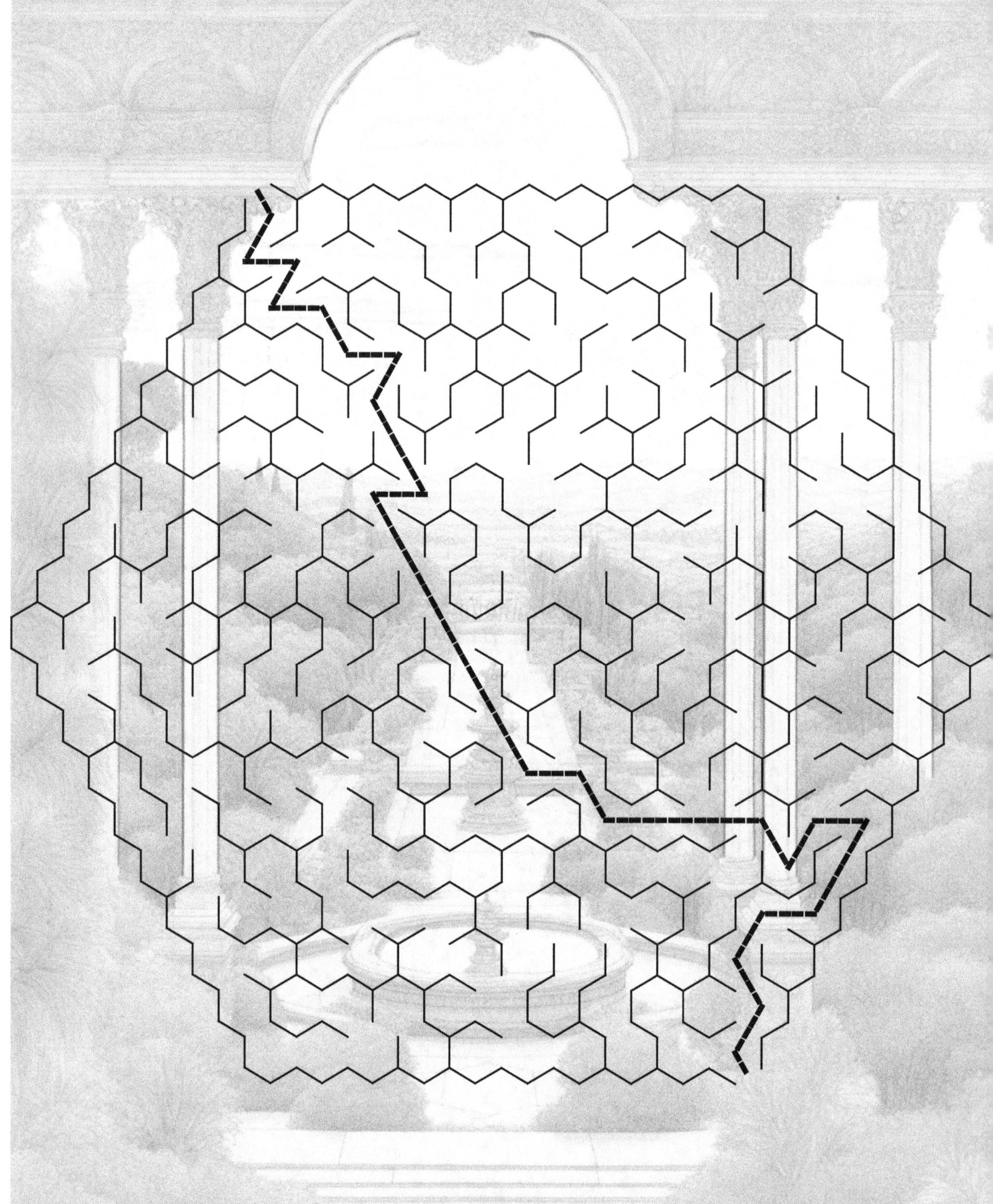

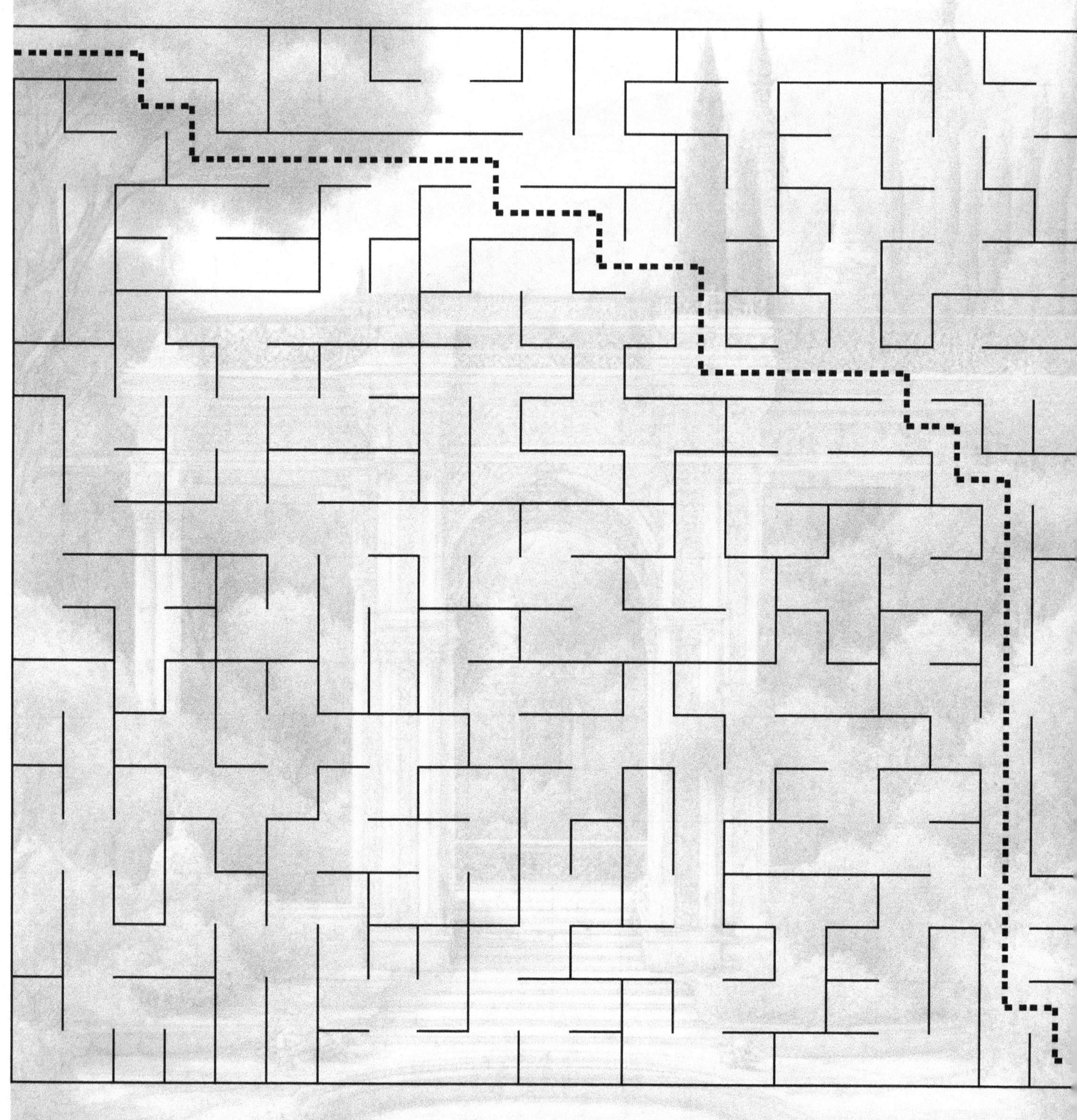

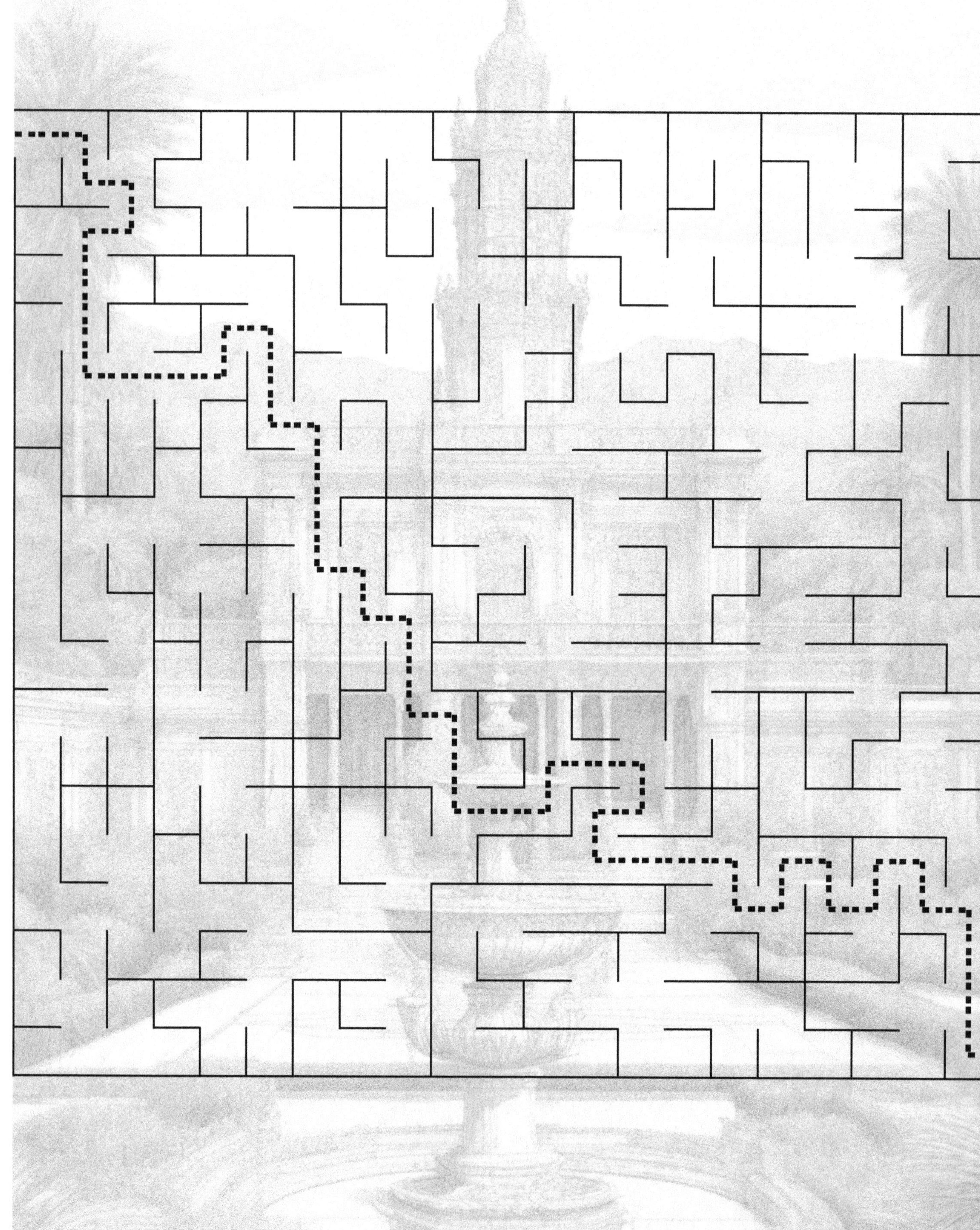

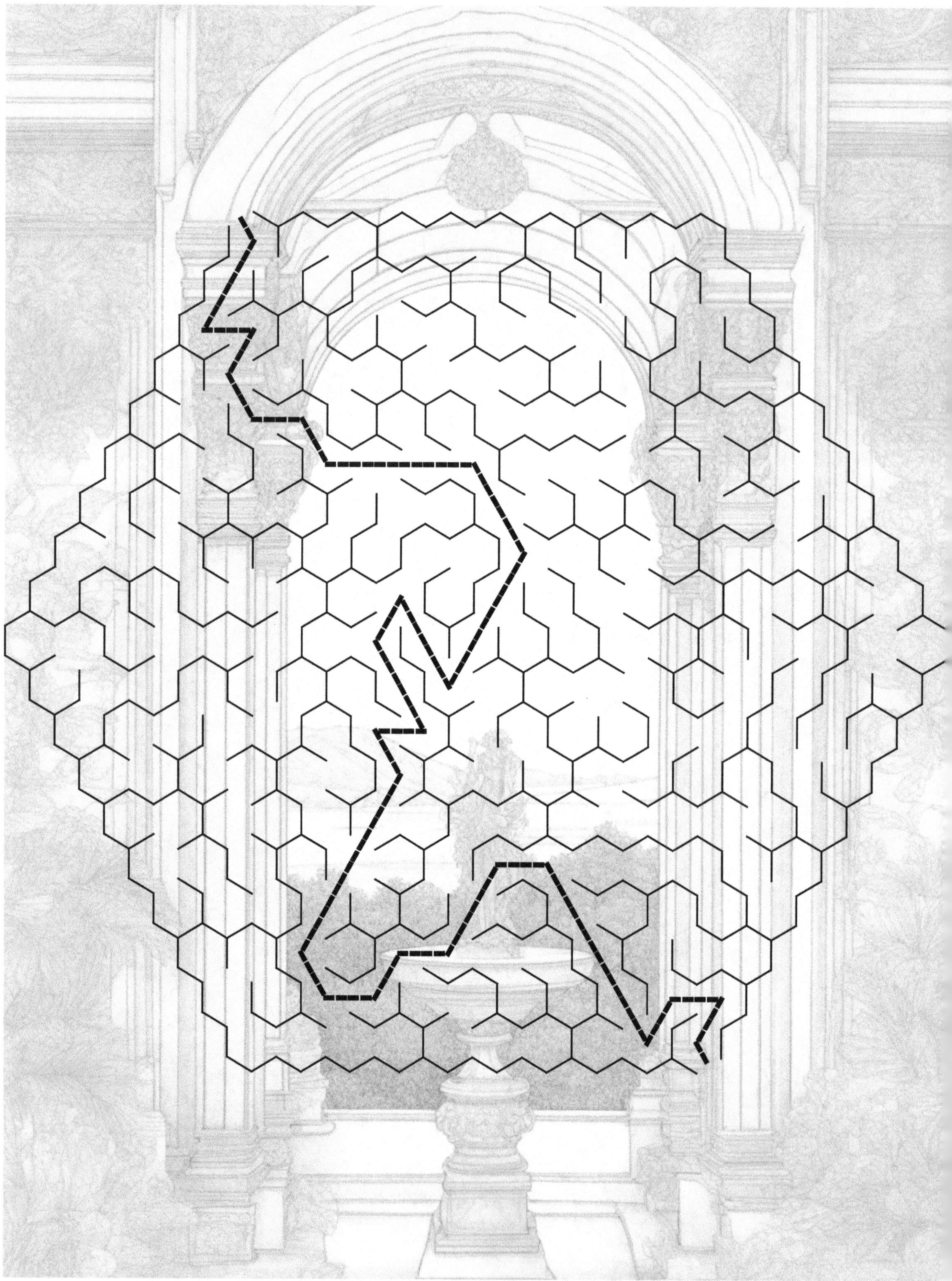

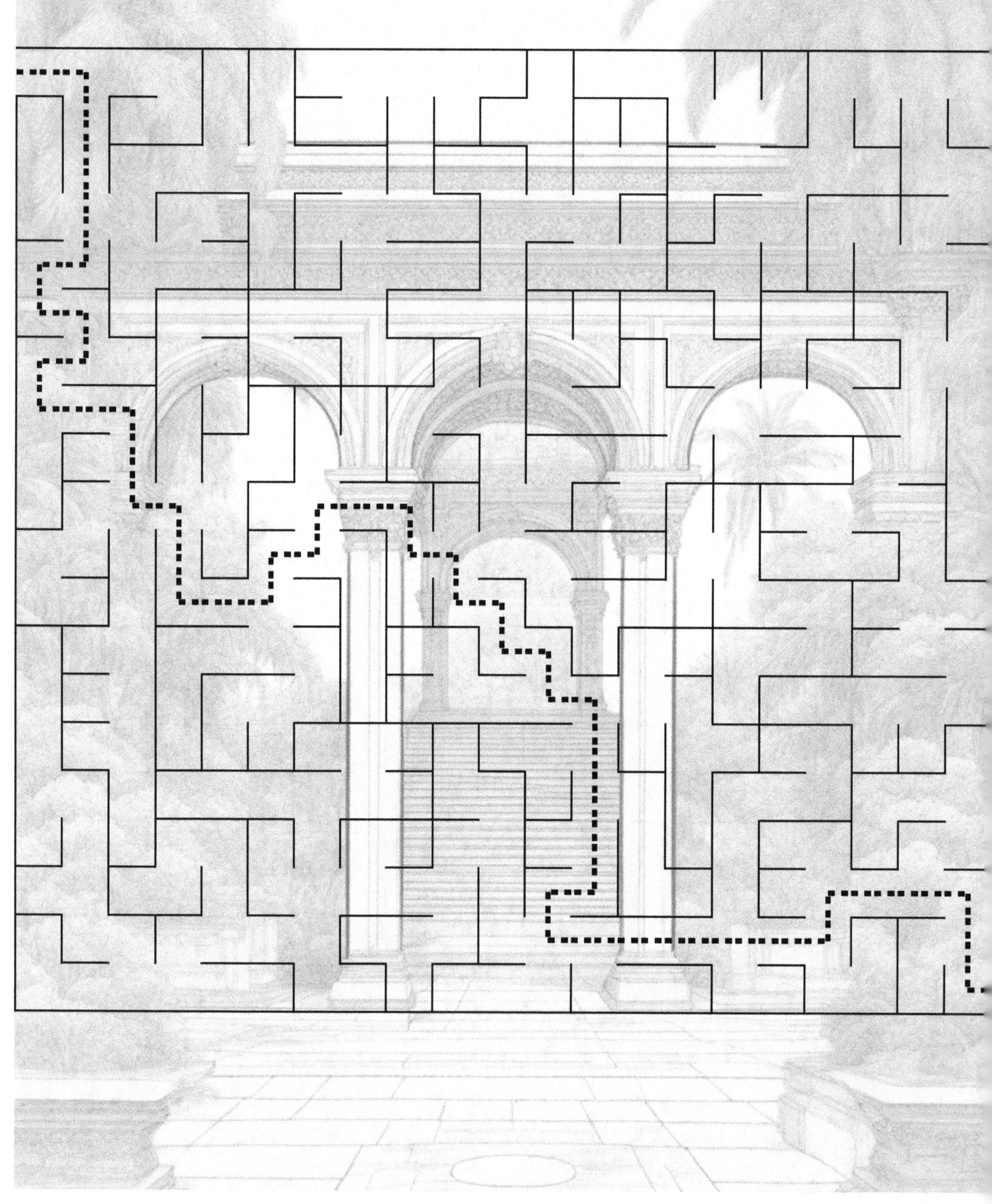

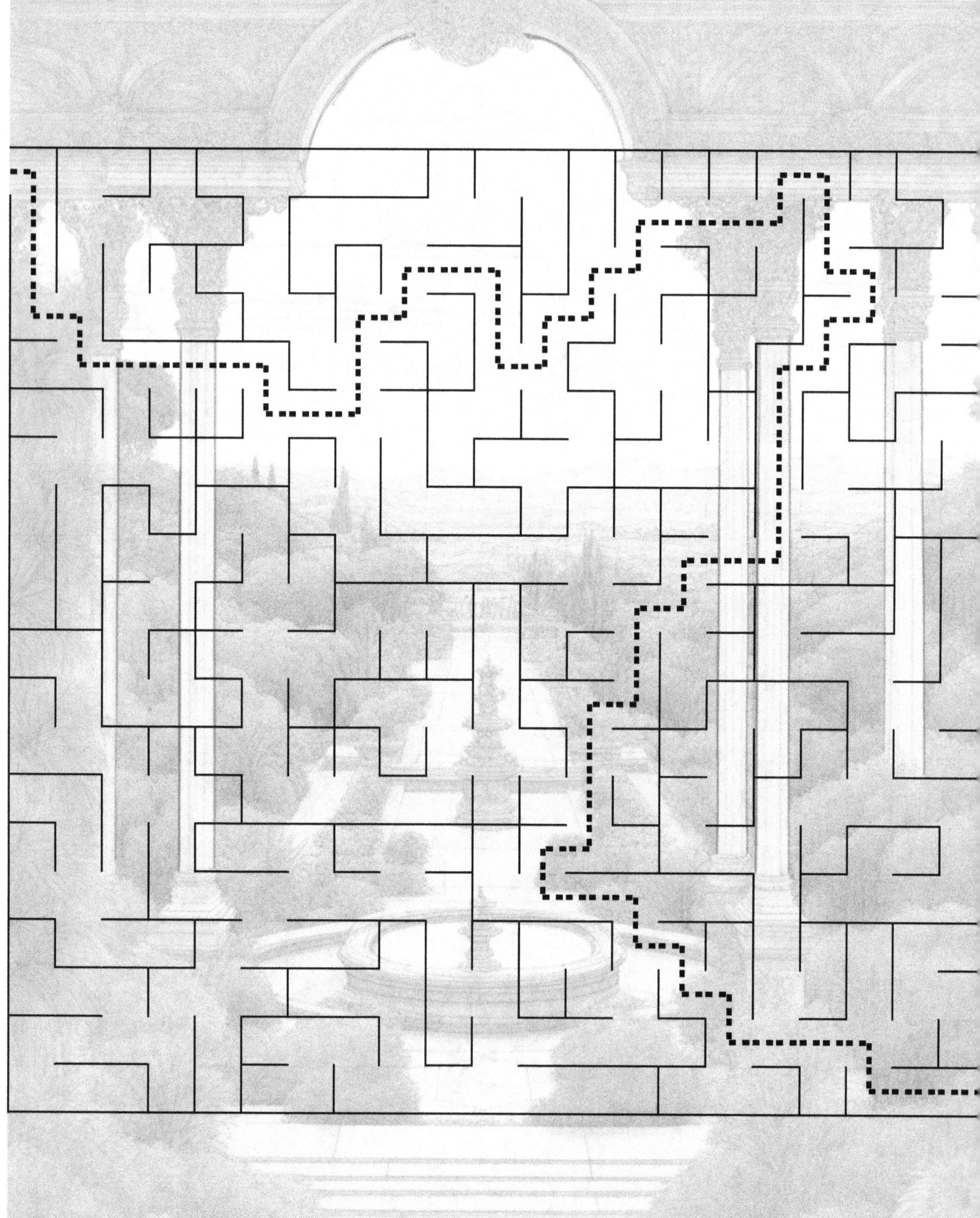

TRACKS & TRUNKS
COLORING BOOK
50 ORIGINAL DESIGNS
FUN FOR ALL AGES!
RELAX & UNWIND
BY ROCK ROULADE COCOON COLLECTIVE

TEDDY BEAR EXPRESS
COLORING BOOK
50 ORIGINAL DESIGNS
RELAX & UNWIND
FUN FOR ALL AGES!
BY ROCK ROULADE COCOON COLLECTIVE

ROYAL RAIL
Retreat
COLORING BOOK
50 ORIGINAL DESIGNS
FUN FOR ALL AGES!
RELAX & UNWIND
BY ROCK ROULADE COCOON COLLECTIVE

TROLLY TOWN
Coloring Book
50 ORIGINAL DESIGNS
FUN FOR ALL AGES
RELAX & UNWIND
By Rock Roulade Cocoon Collective

www.ingramcontent.com/pod-product-compliance
Lightning Source LLC
Chambersburg PA
CBHW060141120726
48003CB00009B/2972